OPEN SESAME

OPEN SESAME

Creating Wealth Through the Magic of Compounding

John J. Kralik M.D.

ISBN: 0692928294
ISBN 13: 9780692928295

Introduction

Because this is a book about time and the time value of money, I feel qualified to write it, even though it is my first book, and I am getting a late start on my writing career.

In 1943, I was a young man studying marine architecture at MIT. But my career as an engineer ended prematurely when I was drafted into the Army. The boys in my unit and I went into training. We were getting ready for the invasions of Europe and North Africa that ended the Second World War.

One day an officer came to our unit. After we had lined up, he said,

"Anyone who would like to be a doctor should step forward now."

Until that moment, I had never thought of becoming a doctor. But I stepped forward. In the moment, it seemed like a good idea.

I was ordered into a basement office where the officer sat at a desk. After a long wait, he said, "Sit down, son." I sat down.

After another seemingly interminable wait, the officer said to me, "Son, how many siblings do you have?"

"Two," I said, "A brother and a sister."

"Thank you," he said, and went back to his paperwork. There were no further questions. Finally, he looked up and said, "You have passed the test. You're going to medical school."

I had to ask: "How would I have failed?"

"Most boys count themselves in the answer to the question. So, for example, you might have said 'three.' That would have been the wrong answer."

It was an important lesson about the need to count accurately.

The Army sent me to the University of Pennsylvania Medical School. The University of Pennsylvania has a magnificent Medical School. It was Americas first Medical School, founded by Benjamin's Franklin in 1765. I remember how the Dean greeted us there: "We didn't select you, and you didn't choose the University of Pennsylvania. But we are going to do our best to make this next four years the best four years of your life."

From that moment, I studied medicine assiduously. I recognized the privilege the Army had given me. Medicine became my mistress. Drs. Isadore Ravdin, James Hardy, William Osler, and Ambrose Pare became my lodestars. The dean was right. I have never been disappointed. I had found my vocation as a surgeon.

My decision to step forward that day was a fateful one. Most of my friends did not step forward that day. Many of them died in battles in Europe and North Africa. It was a bloody war. I was one of the lucky ones. I would live.

I did well in medical school, and became the head resident at University Hospital in Cleveland, Ohio, my hometown.

I met my wife Rita, who was working as a young nurse there at University Hospital, after moving from her hometown of Niagara Falls. We would have nine children. There are six boys and three girls. If you ask any one of them how many siblings they have, they will answer "eight."

When I left the Army after the Korean War, I set up a medical practice at a Catholic hospital in Garfield Heights, a suburb of Cleveland. There, I built one of the first heart-lung machines. These machines made open-heart surgery possible by allowing the blood to keep circulating, and the patient to stay alive, while we worked on the interior of the heart. We operated on small children who were born with congenital malformations of their hearts and had a great record.

In my lifetime, advances in medical science, including open-heart surgery, have greatly increased the expected length of many of our lives. As a result, we must be prepared to support ourselves financially far beyond the years in which we are able to work at peak efficiency. These advances even lengthened my life, which was saved and prolonged by open-heart surgery in 2004. While I recovered from the heart attack and surgery, I could no longer work at the same pace that I had maintained for so many years. I needed to stop operating. Since then, I have been studying the survival science of making my remaining money work to produce the income I can no longer produce with my hands.

Recently, I celebrated my ninety-third birthday. Survival is something I know something about.

Time can do many cruel things to us. For example, I'm a bit shorter than I was the day I stepped over the line to become a doctor. But we can also make time our ally, an ally that can help us survive comfortably during the latter years of our longer lives.

Using time to your advantage is the survival skill I want to teach you in this book. You will need to do a little math, and you will be asked to try some things that won't sound like fun at first. I hope, however, that when you are done, you will thank me for the magic formula you will learn here, and that it will help you through a long life.

Interest, The Hinge on Which the Door Swings

"An investment in knowledge pays the best interest."

—BENJAMIN FRANKLIN.

Big doors swing on little hinges. We often force our entire effort on the door, without realizing the importance of the hinges.

In the same way, we are often focused on what we view as the "principal" issues of our finances: How much will we lend or borrow?

We think we are focusing and the main issues, and, as a result, many of us do not pay attention to how much the interest on the principal adds cost to our lives. Interest may seem like a little hinge when you are negotiating about the principal, but a lot of money hangs on your understanding how it works.

Paying attention to the way interest works will help you stop letting others take advantage of your hard work. Learning to make interest work for you rather than against you will help you survive.

———∞∞∞———

WHAT IS INTEREST?

Interest is a payment to use money. It can be what you pay to use someone else's money. Or what someone else pays you to use your money.

Interest is a little hinge that can swing open big doors for you in your life.

WHAT IS A COMPOUND INTEREST LOAN?

Compound interest loans are loans in which the interest earned is added to the principal repeatedly, at regular intervals. After each of the pre-set periods, the interest is "compounded." What that means is that the interest earned during the just-expired period of time is added to the principal. Then, the holder of the loan earns interest on the new amount: interest on interest.

In a compound interest loan, the total amount of interest earned increases every time the interest is compounded. When you put your money in a long-term investment, such as a certificate of deposit, you are making a compound-interest loan to the bank.

WHY IS COMPOUNDING SO IMPORTANT?

Compound interest is among the most powerful forces in the financial universe. Compounding is a fundamental way to gain wealth.

The idea of compounding interest has been around for 12,000 years. It began when man first planted seeds and started to farm for his food.

The compounding of interest should be a matter of great concern to all of us in our daily lives because it greatly affects every one of us, even if we do not borrow money ourselves. Compounding affects simple loans, mortgages, and our national debt.

The number of compounding periods each year makes a great difference in determining the cost or profit from a loan. The greater the number of compounding periods, the greater the expense of the loan to the borrower, and the greater the profit to the lender. When the number of compounding periods is fewer, the expense of the loan, and the earnings to the lender, are both less.

Interest may be converted into principal by compounding annually, semi-annually, quarterly, monthly, weekly, daily, or continuously.

Interest is usually expressed in a percentage. For example, you might hear of an automobile dealer offering to loan money at 6%. Most people assume this means the percentage charged for a year. The number of times that simple loan like a car loan is compounded can make the real cost of the money much more. And that can make all the difference.

The Compounding Formula and How it Works

"It's a great country, but you can't live in it for nothing."

—WILL ROGERS

To keep living well even after your ability to earn diminishes, you will need to learn the importance of Compounding.

Compounding works through a mathematical formula. To calculate the effect of compounding, you will need to solve this simple mathematical formula.

First, though, to properly use the formula, you will need to know a little about a military sounding term: the Order of Operations.

ORDER OF OPERATIONS

The "Order of Operations" refers to the order in which you perform the various operations that are set forth in a mathematical equation. When I went to grade school, I learned the order of operations through an acronym: **P**lease **E**xcuse **M**y **D**ear **A**unt

Sally. In this acronym, the initial letters of each word stand for **P**arentheses, **E**xponents, **M**ultiplication, **D**ivision, **A**ddition, and **S**ubtraction. Equations are solved, or "factored" by performing the operations of the equation in that order.

It is necessary to use the order of operations in solving the **Compounding Future Value Equation** we are going to learn in this chapter. The compounding equation is simple enough that the order of operations shouldn't worry you too much. Nevertheless, if you sense there is an error in your calculations, this might be a good place to look. Review your order of operations according to the simple acronym I learned so long ago.

The compounding equation is easy to use with small numbers. In the real world, of course, the numbers can get larger.

Don't worry if the compounding equation seems hard to do in your head. Compounding equations are best solved with the use of a scientific or a financial calculator. When I went to school, such calculators did not exist. So we used something you don't see much anymore, a complex three-part ruler called a slide-rule. When my children went to school calculators were prohibitively expensive. They learned the slide-rule too. Scientific and financial calculators are now much more affordable, but can also be found in virtual form on the Internet and used without any expense whatsoever.

For example, calculating a complex fraction or taking the number 1.0125 to the 360th power can be a lot of work when you do it on your own. When you use a scientific calculator, it can be done in an instant. Later, I'll show you how.

THE COMPOUNDING FUTURE VALUE FORMULA

Here's a simple example of how compounding works.

Mary loans John one dollar for a period of one year at 100% interest.

Using the compounding formula, we can figure out the amount that John will owe to Mary at the end of the year. The compounding formula is:

$$A = P \times (1 + r/n)^{nt}$$

In words: A, the accumulated value, equals P, the present value, times (one plus r divided by n) to the n times t power.

In the formula:

- *A is the Accumulated Value*
- *P is the Present Value*
- *r is the interest rate*
- *n is the number of times the loan is compounded each year*
- *t is the duration of the loan in years*

HOW THE FORMULA WORKS.

Let's use our formula on the simple loan between Mary and John.

Here's how the formula works for this case:

$$A = P \times (1 + r/n)^{nt}$$
$$A = 1 \times (1 + 1/1)^{1 \times 1}$$
$$A = \$2$$

To say it in words: A equals 1 times (1+1/1) to the 1 times 1 power. Our Result, A, the accumulated value, equals 2 dollars.

Mary has doubled her money in one year. John isn't too worried. He figures he needed that dollar when he needed it.

That might have been a lot of math for one chapter, but it's about all you need to know to understand the effects of compounding. In the following chapters, we will work the formula through with a few more examples so you can get used to how it can affect the economics of a loan. John and Mary will be with us for a while.

Take Action: Take out a piece of paper and do this for yourself. Use the order of operations. Try it with some more very simple numbers. This will help you get a sense of how the formula works.

3

The Second Lesson: Semi-Annual Compounding

"Interest on debts grows without rain."

—Yiddish Proverb.

Later, after paying back the first dollar, and the additional dollar that Mary earned by lending, John returns to borrow another dollar from Mary. In the meantime, Mary has begun to read this book. She says there will be two periods of compounding. John, who does not have time for books, thinks this sounds reasonable. So. . .

JOHN SEEKS A SECOND LOAN

When he goes to Mary, she tells John that in this second loan the interest will be compounded two times during the period of one year. To use more formal words, it is semiannually compounded. The rate, 100%, is still stated as 1. But the "n" in the compounding formula, the number of times the loan is compounded during the life of the loan, is now 2. The life of the loan is still stated as 1 year, or "1." Now let's see how that comes out.

$$A = P \times (1 + r/n)^{nt}$$
$$A = 1 \times (1 + 1/2)^{2 \times 1}$$
$$A = 1 \times (1.5)^2$$
$$A = \$2.25$$

A, our accumulated value, equals P, the present value, times (1 plus 1/2) to the 2 times 1 power.

When something is taken to the second power it is multiplied by itself once. Here we are multiplying 1.5 times 1.5. A, the accumulated value equals $2.25.

By compounding the loan semi-annually, Mary has earned an extra quarter on her $1 loan. That may sound like a little, but think of it this way: she has increased her profit by 25%!

That's the way compounding works. It makes little changes. These little changes seem to make almost no difference when you examine them in transactions involving small periods of money and small periods of time. But with larger sums of money and the passage of more time, the effect magnifies.

Did Manhattan go for a fair price? Even semi-annual compounding can make money grow at an impressive rate. My wife, Rita, tells me that Dutch settlers purchased Manhattan from the Lenape Indians in 1626 for traded goods valued at 60 guilders, about $24.00. History regards the deal as unconscionable, and indeed it was.

But the deal was 391 years ago. If the Lenape had been able to invest that $24 at 6% interest, compounded semi-annually, $24 would have grown to $262 billion dollars, enough to make them major landowners in today's Manhattan. Unfortunately, there were no bank branches on Manhattan in those days. You do not have the same excuse.

Take Action: Have you ever heard of a loan compounded semi-annually? See if you can find one in your life or experience.

4

The Third Lesson in Compounding:
Quarterly Compounding

*"Interest works day and night in fair weather and foul.
It gnaws at a man's substance with invisible teeth."*

--HENRY WARD BEECHER

John needs still more money and again returns to Mary. Mary has further studied accounting and compounding and tells John that this time there will be four compounding periods. His loan will be compounded quarterly. This sounds like meaningless mumbo-jumbo to John, who readily agrees. The other terms of the loan will be like the previous loans.

Now let's try to figure out what John will owe Mary at the end of the year for his new one dollar loan at 100% interest with four compounding periods.

Remember the formula: *A, the accumulated value, equals P, the present value, times (1+r/n) to the nt power.* Keep saying that until you don't forget it.

Here is how the equation looks as we work through it, using the order of operations.

$$A = P \times (1 + r/n)^{nt}$$
$$A = 1 \times (1 + 1/4)^{1 \times 4}$$
$$A = 1 \times (1.25)^4$$
$$A = \$2.44$$

In words: A equals 1 times (1 plus 1/4) to the 1 x 4 power.

When something is "taken to the 4th power," it is multiplied by itself 4 times. Here, 1.25 x 1.25 x 1.25 x 1.25 = 2.44. A, the accumulated value, equals $2.44. The cost of money continues to rise with the additional compounding.

Take Action: Do you know of any loans in your life that are compounded quarterly?

5

A Fourth Lesson in Compounding: Monthly Compounding

"If a man has money, it is usually a sign that he knows how to take care of it; don't imagine his money is easy to get simply because he has plenty of it."

—EDGAR WATSON HOWE

JOHN SEEKS A FOURTH LOAN.

Again, John returns to Mary for more money. This time Mary says the loan will be compounded on the first day of each month. John thinks that Mary is starting to sound unreasonable. In response, she tells him that she has other customers now, and that is the way of many commercial lenders. She reassures John by saying that the rest of the terms of the loan will be like the first loan she gave to him. John is bored with numbers. He agrees to Mary's terms and goes back to watching television.

Once again John is borrowing $1 at 100% interest. Let's s calculate what John will owe Mary at the end of the year.

Work through the order of operations with me.

$$A = P \times (1 + r/n)^{nt}$$
$$A = 1 \times (1 + 1/12)^{1 \times 12}$$
$$A = 1 \times (1.083)^{12}$$
$$A = \$2.61$$

In words: 1 times (1 plus 1/12) to the 1 times 12 power.

As you can see, this time you will need to multiply 1.083 against itself twelve times to solve the equation.

I learned this sort of calculation when I was a kid, but now financial calculators do it for you.

As we have been going through these equations, I have been using a financial calculator. To "take a number to the power of" another number, enter the number, hit the "yx" button on the calculator, enter the second number, and then hit the "yx" button again.

As I pointed out earlier, there are virtual computers on the internet. So there's no excuse for you not to give it a try. To make it even simpler, you can find calculators on the internet that are fully devoted to compounding. All you need to do is plug in the variables, and the calculator will watch over the equation for you.

I still think it is better that you personally understand the variables, and personally watch how they work in each equation. For this reason, try doing the calculations without a calculator for a while.

When you are done with the equation, you should find that A, the accumulated value, equals $2.61.

Mary is learning to grow her wealth. John is binge-watching a new show on Netflix, and not really cognizant of what is going on. While John may not be noticing, you are, because you are reading this book instead of watching television. So you know that compounding can make a real difference in the profit of lending and the cost of borrowing.

Take action: Do you have any loans in your life that compound monthly? As you have searched out loans that compound at various intervals, consider the economic strength of the parties on each side of the loan. Doesn't it seem like the party with the greater economic strength gets the better of the compounding equation? For example, when the bank loans money for a car loan, does it get better compounding terms than when a depositor loans it money by depositing in a savings account?

TAKE HEART:

When I was young doctor, I joined and supported a very hopeful organization called The Christophers, which was founded by Father James Keller, a charismatic Maryknoll priest who believed that everyone has been given a special task in life. Throughout my life, I have been given many tasks, which have included prolonging the lives of many of God's children, including a few Maryknoll priests. But now, I believe I have been given another task, teaching you to think clearly about compound interest.

The motto Father Keller chose for the Christophers was derived from an old Chinese Proverb: *"It is better to light one candle than to curse the darkness."* These have been good words to live by, and I have taught them to my children. I have tried to light some candles for them to see by.

Do not be discouraged about what you are learning about compound interest, and how it may be working against you at this point in your life. By understanding it, you are taking the first step toward taking advantage of it, instead of letting it take advantage of you.

After you have helped yourself with the knowledge, help someone else avoid the traps it can lay for those who are in weaker financial positions. Light one candle for someone else, and show them the way out of the darkness.

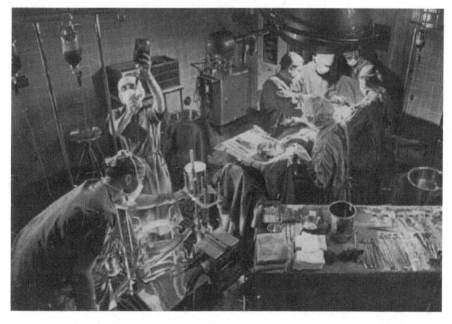

Doing open heart surgery on one of the earliest heart lung machines.

6

A Fifth Lesson in Compounding

"Insanity is repeating the same mistakes and expecting different results."

—NARCOTICS ANONYMOUS

JOHN SEEKS A FIFTH LOAN.

Despite the increasing cost, John is still in the market for a loan. He returns to Mary. She always seems to have money.

Mary has continued her financial literacy studies and tells John that this time the compounding will be daily. When he complains, she tells him that this is the same way it is done for many student loans and some car loans. "At least I'm explaining it to you," she says. "Some lenders just put it in the fine print."

Let's see what John now owes Mary for the one year loan at 100% interest when it is compounded every day. Here are the numbers in the familiar equation:

$$A = P \times (1 + r/n)^{nt}$$
$$A = 1 \times (1 + 1/365)^{1 \times 365}$$
$$A = 1 \times (1.003)^{365}$$
$$A = \$2.71$$

In words: A equals 1 times (1 plus 1/ 365) to the 1 times 365 power. A, the accumulated value, equals $2.71.

Were you able to get your calculator to take something to the 365th power?

Once again, the amount of money Mary earns increases by a large percentage, even though all other variables stay the same.

Have you ever checked into how the bank or credit card company who loans you money is compounding your loan? You should start doing so now. Credit cards will either start out compounding the loan daily, or do so as soon as you fail to turn in one of your monthly payments on time. Very few people can avoid missing a monthly payment date, especially if they have multiple cards or other bills.

Of course, the other elements of the equation are important too: the time, the rate of the interest. But we usually notice these elements. We seldom think about the compounding. It is rarely mentioned in advertisements for loans. I hope you won't ever borrow money again without considering this part of the equation. The lender certainly considers it.

So far in our story the lender has been on the "A side" of the equation. Later, I will discuss a few ideas that may help you to get to the "A side" of the equation. I think you are beginning to realize that is where you want to be.

Take Action: Try to gain an understanding of how every loan in your life is compounded. You might be surprised.

7

The Eighth Wonder of the World

"'The best thing for being sad,' replied Merlyn, beginning to puff and blow, 'is to learn something. That is the only thing that never fails.'"

—T.H. White, The Once and Future King.

Not all grammar schools teach financial literacy. In fact, many people go through their entire education without learning it because they are more fascinated by other, seemingly more intellectual pursuits. Like social media. As a result, the lack of financial literacy handicaps many of us for life.

In fact, financial literacy is a key to your survival over a long life. If you learn to manage your money now, you will thank me when you are ninety-three.

The best time to start learning about your money was twenty years ago. The next best time is today. As Merlyn noted in T.H. White's wonderful book, learning something new is a perfect remedy for feeling sad. I have gone to this remedy during the many times of sadness that inevitably occur in a life as long as mine.

Understanding compounding and the time value of money is a good place to begin your financial literacy.

A dollar today is more valuable than a dollar next year because the dollar today has the potential to earn interest and increase in value. Think of it as an ordinary tree that can grow into a money tree if managed carefully.

Compounding is standard business practice in our country and is attached to most all loans and mortgages in addition to the normal interest rate. Many common loans are compounded daily. The more times a loan is compounded the greater the expense.

Compounding is the accumulation of the time value of money. Relatively few people understand it properly. Eight people who have focused on this formula now own the same wealth as half of the world's population - 7 1/2 billion people.

Albert Einstein, who wrote many formulas far more complex than the compounding formula, is believed to have said,

"He who understands interest earns it. He who doesn't understand it pays it. It is the eighth wonder of the ancient world."

Whether he actually said this can be disputed, but the fact that the wisdom of the quote is attributed to an archetype of intellect tells you that the generations that followed him have seen the wisdom of these words.

Take Action: How do I change myself from someone who pays interest to someone who earns it? This is a difficult proposition, but I have a few ideas for you. Mark Twain said:

"The secret of getting ahead is getting started."

Let's get started.

8

Getting on the Right Side of the Compounding Equation

"It's far better to buy a wonderful company at a fair price than a fair company at a wonderful price."

— WARREN BUFFETT

Warren Buffett believes in accumulating and reinvesting. He thrives through the time value of money. You can bet that Warren Buffett knows all about compounding. In fact, he owns a few banks. He knows that you must be on the A side of the compounding equation, where the Accumulated Value starts piling up.

Mr. Buffett likes to tell a story about Coca-Cola that illustrates the power of compounding. The example he uses is the reinvestment value of dividends in Coca-Cola stock.

Coca-Cola became a public corporation in 1919. If you had purchased $40 worth of Coca-Cola stock in 1919, and reinvested the dividends, it would be worth considerably more today. As a matter of fact, your $40 would now be worth $11.5 million. No wonder compounding is referred to as the eighth wonder of the world.

To repeat this amazing transaction today would require a purchase of $400 of Coca Cola stock at a discount brokerage, or a Dividend Reinvestment Program Account that will reinvest the dividends, which are paid four times a year.

Of course, you will need to live a considerable amount of time. Figure out how long that would be.

Mr. Buffett likes to drink Coca-Cola, and for him, it has worked out. Every person is different, however, and for the average person Coca-Cola is a less-than-healthful beverage choice.

When it comes to financial behavior, Mr. Buffett is an excellent role model. When it comes to your health, I suggest that you listen to your doctor.

GETTING STARTED WITH A DIVIDEND REINVESTMENT PROGRAM, OR "DRIP"

One simple way to start compounding your money is to go directly to the investor relations web site of the company you wish to purchase. As an example, search "Coca Cola investor relations." You will need to move through several screens and eventually get to the "Initial enrollment plan" application.

After you invest a small amount of principal, the company will take your dividends and re-invest them each time they are paid. When you get and reinvest dividends four times a year you are on the left side of the compounding equation. If the market value of the asset increases, you will win there too. Normally, a good company will pay dividends and compound your money four times each year. A good company will also increase in value over time because as the world's population grows so will its sales—so long as people want the product.

A DRIP is a simple way to gain financial resources without much effort.

Be patient. Take care of your health. Your money is being compounded for later enjoyment.

The Warren Buffett stock portfolio contains 400,000,000 shares of Coca-Cola stock. It has been compounding for a long time.

Take Action: Take $400 and open a dividend reinvestment program account with a company that you think will be around for a long time.

Mr. Buffett probably chose Coca Cola because he liked the drink and he looked around and saw that a lot of other people did too. Choose a company that you consider vital to the way you live your life or the way you do business. Ask yourself, "How long do you expect that you and other people will continue to use that product?"

For example, there has been a recent run up in Amazon stock. How often are you shopping at Amazon, or one of the many companies that it owns? Is that a trend you expect to continue? In contrast, there has been a recent fall-off of the stocks of many retailers. How often are you going to the mall lately? How does that compare to what you and your family did ten years ago?

9

The Importance of Keeping Track

"The number one problem in today's generation and economy is the lack of financial literacy."

—ALAN GREENSPAN

LEDGER A.

I n 1851, the family of John D. Rockefeller had just moved to Owego, New York. John D. Rockefeller was 12 years old. Even at this age, he frequently assumed the financial responsibility for his family because his father spent long periods of time away from home. The young lad budgeted family expenses and was frugal in his activities.

A long remembered story tells of young Rockefeller's experience digging potatoes and loaning money to a neighboring farmer. Rockefeller was paid 37 cents a day for digging the potatoes. After saving his money from this labor, he loaned $50 to a neighbor at 7 percent interest. After a period of one year, he collected the $50. . . and 3 1/2 dollars' interest. He was amazed that he could earn money without manual labor! He was never seen digging potatoes again.

At age 16, Rockefeller began conscientiously recording his personal expenses and income in a journal that he named "Ledger A." The journal was a small red book that he purchased for $.10. Copies of Ledger A have been preserved and are an accurate record of young Rockefeller's receipts and expenditures. The idea of accurately recording your receipts and expenditures remains to this day a very excellent financial discipline.

John D. Rockefeller was very proud of his bookkeeping capabilities and encouraged his associates to study accounting and bookkeeping.

Accounting matters! If you wish to have a good measure of financial independence, study bookkeeping and accounting. One or two semesters of study at college should be enough. Whatever else you do with your life, those semesters will serve you well throughout your life.

THE FLYING CLOUD DIET

In the 1970's I learned that the keeping close track of anything can help you take control of it. As a heart surgeon, I had many patients who were overweight. To encourage them to take control of their diet, I told them to get a journal and write down everything that they were eating. I also told them to buy a special setting of china, and eat everything off that set of china.

Because they had to take out their complete set of china (instead of just eating the food in the paper in which it came) my patients had to stop and think about what they were doing. Instead of just grabbing a bag of potato chips and taking out a few handfuls, they needed to take out their china, and place the potato chips on the plate. That gave them time to think. Was this really something that they should eat, or were they eating to pass the time or because of an emotional reaction to something that had just happened?

Then, after they had eaten, my patients had to write down what they had eaten and be accountable for it. This allowed them to see when they had already passed the daily requirement of calories that was required to sustain their present weight. They would have this in mind while they washed the china and placed it in its carrying case. I hoped that they would still have it in mind when they next sat down to eat.

Most of my patients lost weight because using the special set of china allowed them to get control of their eating. Many were saved from the necessity of one of my surgeries to unblock their coronary arteries.

Don't get me wrong, I loved operating. It allowed me to use the talent that I had spent years of training to develop. But I knew that it would be better for my patients to avoid my knife, especially after I had operated on them already.

Because I wanted to see if my theories on eating worked, I tried my own diet. Because I liked a china pattern called "Flying Cloud," I bought a set of china in that pattern, as well as a little case to carry it around. I wanted to show my patients that the process was feasible. I called my diet the "Flying Cloud Diet."

I lost quite a bit of weight following that diet.

Today, there are many "apps" that allow you to track what you are eating or spending on your phone. Even so, the best way to do this, and the most effective way to lose weight, is to take out a pencil and paper and write it down. It might be hard for people, but the effort and thought become a habit, and after a while you may not need the pencil or paper or china anymore. It will always be there if you feel you are going through a bad period and you willpower is challenged.

Managing your money is much the same as tracking your calories. By tracking what you spend and earn, you will become more self-aware and make better decisions. Your financial fitness will improve each month.

THE CHECKING ACCOUNT, YOUR FIRST LEDGER A.

Your first Ledger A will probably be your checking account. There is one account. Whenever you withdraw money from the ATM, or use your debit card, or write a check, the balance is reduced. Sometimes the bank makes a charge that you forgot you agreed to when you signed up. When your paycheck is deposited, the balance goes up.

Most people do not pay attention to each individual event that affects their financial condition. They hope for the best, and are shocked when things turn out badly. This is not entirely their fault. For example, advertising reinforces the notion that we are entitled to eat out, to drive a brand new car, and to wear new clothes at all times. Each time we spend money without keeping track, say with a credit card, a bank somewhere is making money.

It is much better to keep your own ledger, in your checkbook, or in what you should call your first Ledger A. This will give you a physical, tactile awareness of each dollar you spend in the same way that I wanted my patients to have a physical, tactile awareness of each calorie they added. Just by taking this action, you will increase your financial awareness, and improve your financial condition, just as my patients' physical condition improved.

DOUBLE ENTRY BOOKKEEPING.

A checking account is an example of single-entry bookkeeping. Most people with an elementary education can comprehend single-entry bookkeeping, because it is just arithmetic. But it is an incomplete picture of your financial condition.

As you go through life, it is my hope that you will meet with success—especially after you learn the secret of compounding. As a result, you will have a financial condition that is composed of assets and liabilities in addition to your checking account.

I urge you take accounting early in your life so that you can comprehend, and practice, double-entry book keeping. In double-entry bookkeeping, every financial transaction is both a debit and a credit to the overall financial equation that depicts your financial position, or net worth. Teaching you double-entry bookkeeping is beyond the scope of this book, but I want to explain to you how it works, so I can encourage you to start doing it early in life.

The most important business document in double-entry bookkeeping is the General Journal. Accountants call the General Journal the journal of first entry. It contains all of an organization's financial transactions. Entries are made in chronological order from bills and source documents. It is kept along with the receipts and bills so that the authenticity of entries can be easily checked.

The practice of keeping a general journal for revenue and expenditures is not new. There is more than 500 years of experience. The bookkeepers of Venice were making entries in their general journals in 1492 when Columbus discovered America.

There are special forms for keeping the general journal records. These forms are all quite similar and can be found in all accounting books. Keeping a general journal is the first step in the accounting cycle. It is a priority procedure.

In double-entry bookkeeping, there is a debit and credit entry for all transactions. For example, a payment for groceries will represent a debit to the asset account that tracks the cash in my bank account. It will also represent a credit to the expense account that tracks the amount I am spending on groceries. Both the debit and the credit are recorded in the general journal.

From the general journal, accountants prepare the ledgers for each individual account. If there is no general journal it is not possible to keep an accurate ledger. When there are questions as to the authenticity of a ledger entry, the general journal is used to check the transaction. When a transaction is transferred from the general journal to the ledger, the general journal is marked in such a way that will prevent a repeat recording of the transaction.

All reliable businesses keep a general journal. Most successful individuals and families you know keep general journals to record their financial transactions. Join them.

All students should have an up to-date general journal before graduating from high school. If you are a college student, don't go off to school without first learning how to maintain a general journal. If you are a college president or the head of a corporation, you may want to spend time examining your organization's general journal. Throughout his life, John D. Rockefeller spent time checking his bookkeepers.

General journal transactions should be recorded promptly. If you wait more than 24 hours, much of the value of keeping a general journal is lost. Get rid of the old shoe box, sit down and promptly record your transactions in a general journal. If you get sophisticated about this, there are ways to image the source documents so that you can always find them if you need them.

In the United States the middle class is rapidly disappearing. Politicians and the news media are full of divisive explanations for this. If you want to make your own life better, learn double-entry bookkeeping, and record all of your transactions in a general journal.

Take Action: Start your own "Schedule A." There can be many different forms that this will eventually take, but just get a sheet of graph paper and write every transaction you have for a month. Then decide which of the many commercially available products for keeping track might be best for you.

The second step is to take an accounting course. Then move your system from a single-entry to a double entry system.

John D. Rockefeller understood the power of education. In 1890, he helped found the University of Chicago with an investment of $600,000, which is the equivalent of $25 million in today's dollars. He often said that this was the best invest-ment that he ever made.

Accounting courses are available at the Chicago Booth School of Business—though you needn't go to those lengths to find them. A perfectly good accounting course is probably available at your local community college.

10

Keeping Track of the Economy

"It is well enough that people of the nation do not understand our banking and monetary system. If they did, I believe there would be a revolution before tomorrow morning."

--HENRY FORD

A well-run life has well-kept accounting books. A well-run company must have good accounting books. Even countries must keep track somehow. How else will we know whether the country is succeeding?

President Donald Trump frequently mentions the GDP, the Gross Domestic Product. It is a closely watched economic indicator, a measurement of business activity as provided by the US Department of Commerce. Four business factors are evaluated to make this report: consumption, investments, government expenditure, and balance of imports and exports.

Here is the government's GDP report for a quarter during which I was writing this book:

"**Quarterly data:** Real gross domestic product increased at an annual rate of 3.2 percent in the third quarter of 2016, according to the "second" estimate released by the Bureau of Economic Analysis. In the second quarter, real GDP increased 1.4 percent."

Because the 3rd quarter 2016 report showed strong GDP growth, the Federal Reserve decided to raise interest rates. The stock market seemed encouraged, and the market averages rose. Stocks had record prices.

The GDP reports are easily obtained over the internet and are not difficult to understand. People managing money evaluate this report much as a good driver checks the gas in his tank before going on a long automobile trip.

A 3-4% growth rate for the United States' GDP is considered very satisfactory. Mr. Trump heavily criticized President Obama for failing to steward the country toward such growth, and his criticism resonated—even though the economy was headed towards 3% just before the election. Nevertheless, Mr. Trump successfully argued that Hillary Clinton would bring more of the same sluggish growth.

Mr. Trump seems to have a lot of confidence in his assertions that he can do better. Why not keep track and see how he is doing? Check the GDP. It might help you decide how to vote next time.

Take Action: Track the GDP for President Trump's first term. Compare it to President Obama's second term. Do you think either President is responsible for what has happened? What other forces are at work either causing or preventing economic growth?

Understanding the state of the overall economy will help you make sound investment decisions. Remember, however, that you cannot control the events that shape an economy as large as that in this country. You can only keep your own set of books in order, your own budget balanced.

11

When the Numbers Get Big
Borrowing Gets Unconscionable

"Eighty per cent of your success comes from twenty per cent of your efforts. The 'vital few' and the 'trivial many' are recurrent entities."

--PARETO PRINCIPLE

In the first few chapters, we learned the compounding formula by applying it to a simple $1 loan. That was an easy way to show you how to do the math. But most loans are much bigger than that.

JOHN'S BIGGEST LOAN YET.

Let's assume that John wants to borrow a sum of money that he can use to buy something substantial: a new suit. He goes to Mary and asks her to borrow $1000. Even in 2016, you can still get a decent suit for that. Mary is always agreeable when she sees a way to earn a little extra cash, and John has been a good credit risk. She tells John that she will loan him $1000 for two years at 12% interest. In real life, you might be able to get a rate like that. The loan will be compounded semiannually. How much will John owe Mary at the end of two years?

We will use the compounding formula. Do you remember it?

$$A = P \times (1 + r/n)^{nt}$$

A equals P times (one plus r/n) to the nt power.
Remember:
A *equals the Accumulated Value*
P *equals Present Value*
r *equals interest rate in decimals*
n *equals number compounding periods each year*
t *equals number of years*
Now our problem:

A equals 1000 times (1 plus .12/2) to the
2 x 2 power.
$$A = 1000 \times (1 + .12/2)^{2 \times 2}$$
A equals 1000 x (1.06) to the 4th power.
$$A = 1000 \times (1.06)^4$$
A equals \$1,262.48
$$A = \$1,262$$

John owes Mary \$1,262.48 at the end of the second year. The compound interest is

\$1262.48 - \$1000 equals \$262.48

Mary has earned $262.48. Pretty good for a $1,000 investment over 2 years.

JOHN'S LONGEST LOAN: PAYING OVER THIRTY YEARS SOUNDS GOOD AT FIRST

Like most people in the United States, John lives largely on borrowed money. He returns to Mary and asks for another loan. Mary lives more frugally and can loan John $1000 for a period of 30 years.

Really? 30 years? That might sound a little crazy at first, but 30 years is about the term of the mortgages that nearly everyone uses to buy their homes.

Mary agrees to make this loan at 15% interest, compounded every 30 days. This too might seem crazy, but interest rates on 30-year mortgages have gone as high as 18% in my lifetime. People borrowing on secondary markets because their credit is bad might pay even more.

Let's see what John owes Mary at the end of 30 years for the use of just $1,000. First, try doing it by yourself. I'll bet you can do it. If you get stuck, you can always return to the book, and then we'll go through it in words and numbers together.

Ok, here goes.

$$(\text{A equals 1000 times (1 plus .15/12)} \\ \text{to the 30} \times \text{12 power.})$$
$$A = 1000 \times (1 + .0125)^{30 \times 12}$$
$$(\text{A equals 1000 times (1 plus .0125)} \\ \text{to the 360 power.})$$

$$A = 1000 \times (1.0125)^{360}$$
$$(A \text{ equals } 1000 \times 87.5409)$$
$$A = 1000 \times 87.5409$$
$$A = \$87{,}540.90$$

John borrowed $1,000, but pays back $87,540. Hardly a good deal. It probably wouldn't surprise you to know that millions of Americans routinely make similar bargains, almost without thinking. We make this choice because we think it is the normal way, the way everyone else does things.

John should've listened to the advice of his mother and learned to live without resorting to borrowed money.

At one time, we learned these principals of thrift from our parents, from our church, from books of wisdom like the Bible. I grew up during the Great Depression in the United States. So I often heard the following old Scottish Proverb: "Willful waste makes woeful want." We were acutely aware that wasting something in the moment would result in a later need. We now live in an era when we are overwhelmed by advertising that tells us the opposite, and we are worse off for it.

We know the better way, yet we all keep making the same mistakes. Why?

Try This Instead: Find some part of your daily routine where you are "wasting" money. Cable television anyone? Can you brew your own coffee? Use a teabag twice? Try to change one routine.

Become one of the "vital few."

12

Dividends: a Get Rich Scheme for Anyone

"You miss 100 percent of the shots you never take."

—WAYNE GRETZKY

Miles D. White, chairman and CEO of Abbott Laboratories tells the story of a secretary named Grace. As a secretary, Grace was not at the top of the corporate ladder. But four years into her job, she purchased three shares of company stock for just under $200. She held on to those three shares.

Those three shares alone made her a multimillionaire. Through the company dividend — and the miracle of compounding — she died with a $7 million fortune.

Grace wasn't abnormally lucky. Any investor who bought $1,000 worth of high-dividend-paying stock 75 years ago would have about $3,000,000 today,

Yes the latest conventional wisdom on Wall Street pegs dividend-paying stocks as overvalued. Such "wisdom" is usually wrong. Ordinary investors and Wall Street gurus alike have long favored dividend-paying stocks for their steady returns. For most Americans, they remain among the surest paths to wealth. But watch out: If the company stops paying a dividend, then maybe it has become overvalued or run into some other kind of trouble. This should make you consider shifting your investment to a better company. Later, I will teach you some simple steps for how to evaluate the health of your investments.

Most large companies share their profits with stockholders by paying cash "dividends," typically once every three months. Dividends range from a few pennies to a dollar or more for every share. Shareholders can pocket this cash or reinvest it to buy more of the company's stock. If they choose the latter, they'll own more shares and thus earn even more in dividends down the road. Usually, the cost of purchasing these additional shares is less than the cost you pay going through a broker.

Reinvesting essentially creates a snowball effect. As the years roll on, a small investment can yield a huge return. In fact, from 1930 to 2012, dividends accounted for 42% of the total return of the S&P 500 stock market index, according to a Morgan Stanley study.

Dividend stocks are typically far less risky than those with no payout. After all, it takes discipline, stability and a healthy outlook for the future to maintain those regular payments.

As I write this, my wife Rita is coming up upon her 90th birthday. When our nine children were young, she purchased each of them a few shares of AT&T Corporation, and placed them in dividend reinvestment programs. In the early 1980's, AT&T split into nine different corporations. Now my children were invested in nine different dividend reinvestment programs. This made 81 total investments. A $1,250 investment in AT&T corporation from that era would now be worth more than $40,000 today, without compounding. Most of my children sold these investments throughout their life, sometimes for necessities. If they had saved them until today, they would represent a retirement account the size of many people's 401k accounts.

In 1985 we deposited $5,000 in each of two New Zealand Banks. It has grown in value so that presently it amounts to $101,000.

Take Action: Take a few shots at wealth. Try buying 5 shares of 5 stocks in companies that pay regular dividends through their dividend reinvestment programs. Give them 10 years, and see what happens.

If you are in your sixties, remember, it is not too late. If you happen to be as lucky as I am, you have another thirty years of compounding ahead. Think of St. Paul's advice:

> *"Give no thought to what lies behind but push on to what is ahead."*

> SAINT PAUL, PHIL. 3, 8-14.

Walking with my wife Rita on the beach today. Walking stretches out your life. Compound interest stretches out your finances.

13

Taking the Vital Signs

"The lack of money is the root of all evil."

--MARK TWAIN

When you visit your doctor—whether in in Chicago, New York or Miami-- the first 10 minutes are quite similar. The nurse will weigh you, measure your height, the circumference of your neck, take your blood pressure, determine your heart rate, and check your respiration. Collectively these determinations are called your vital signs. The nurse will file your vital signs so that on future visits comparisons can be made.

Those who are successful at finance make similar determination when they evaluate investments. Taking financial vital signs is a little less organized than in medicine but the process is very important.

VITAL SIGN ONE: FREE CASH FLOW

Free cash flow is one vital sign that the experts never omit. The numbers used to calculate free cash flow are found on the cash flow statement that all public companies publish. Major corporations usually publish a cash flow statement every three months. You can find it on the Internet.

To determine the free cash flow, we need another formula. You subtract capital expenditures and dividends from the item identified as cash flow from operations. You can find all three of these determinations listed on the cash flow statement.

Free cash flow is like a solvency ratio that tells you about the company's ability to operate. You can compare free cash flow to the song "When I was single and my pockets did jingle." It is cash that the president and Board of Directors can use to engage in new activities at the end of the quarter or at the end of the year. They may use this money to increase wages, to increase dividend, to buy back shares of their stock or perhaps to purchase a subsidiary corporation.

Just as the physician compares your vital signs from each of your visits to see trends in your health, the financial analyst compares the amount of free cash flow from quarter-to-quarter and from year-to-year. It is a very effective way to determine the vitality and solvency of a corporation. Warren Buffett has popularized this determination.

VITAL SIGN TWO: CASH FLOW PERCENTAGE

Because you would expect large corporations to have more free cash flow than small corporations, there is a second step to this determination. This second step gives you a way to measure how a company is doing for a company of its size. This is determining the cash-flow percentage.

To determine the cash-flow percentage, you divide the free cash flow by the market capitalization, another figure available on the financial report. This will give you the cash flow percentage. A good cash flow percentage is in the range six or seven per cent.

VITAL SIGN THREE: NET PROFIT MARGIN

Net Profit Margin is another important ratio that is easy to understand. Profit margin is the percentage of revenue that a company keeps as profit. It is obtained by dividing net income by net sales.

Most large corporations post their Net Profit Margin four times a year. These values are easily obtained over the Internet. As an example, Coca-Cola's net profit margin in 2016 was 16.6%, and Apple's was 19.6%.

Exxon: 4.52%

Microsoft: 22.93%

Amgen: 34.71%

McDonalds: 19.85 %

A substantial net profit margin is an indication that a company has a product with a durable competitive advantage. All of these stocks are good companies, but now you have a way of comparing them.

Take Action: Take the Three Vital Signs of each of your Investments. If they do not tell a good story, consider investing in a company with better vital signs.

14

Getting More Money

"A hundred times every day I remind myself that my inner and outer life depend on the labours of other men, living and dead, and that I must exert myself in order to give in the same measure as I have received."

-- ALBERT EINSTEIN

Everyone would like to be on the A side of the equation, but before you invest, you need money. Many of us feel we need all of the money we have just to get by. How, you are asking, do you find money for investing? First, don't give up. You have asked a very important question.

There are two major ways to begin assembling money. These ways depend on you and your effort rather than on luck. You will find that most people who have money started out by these methods. Luck came later.

The two ways are:

1. You can earn more money or
2. You can learn to save more money.

Both of these are important, and you should consider your life in view of these efforts every day.

Of course, people get money in other ways—winning the lottery for example. But these are less common. And when people get money without learning how to earn it and preserve it, they often lose it quickly.

Even people who are working hard may find their wages have become stagnant because of forces outside their control. In such cases, it is important to consider saving. After my heart attack made me retire, I focussed mainly on saving to find new money to invest.

But where do we save? The Pareto principle quoted at the beginning of Chapter 11 has guided many people who have had success in saving more money.

Pareto was an Italian economist and mathematician. His study determined that 80% of the wealth in Italy was owned by 20% percent of the people. He was also a gardener and cultivated peas in his vegetable garden. After examining his harvest, he determined that 80% of-the peas came from 20% of the pods. It was the beginning of the 80/20 principle which applies to many diverse situations. 80% of the effects come from 20% of the causes.

The 80/20 principle applies to most of our expenditures. 80% are trivial and 20% are vital. By limiting many of the 80% trivial expenditures you can save money for investing.

In 1924, John D. Rockefeller was the world's richest man. He was 85 years old, retired and living in Ormond Beach Florida. There are some cold days and nights at Ormond Beach during the months of December, January and February. During those cold days Rockefeller loved to sit in front of his wood burning fireplace. One day when his butler Michael was present he inquired of Michael the length of the logs in the fireplace. They were 12 inches in length. "Don't you think we could have the same fire and warmth if the logs were only 10 inches long?" he inquired of Michael. So in the future the logs were 10 inches in length. Rockefeller was proud of his achievement. Rockefeller had difficulty passing on this frugal quality to his children. Probably because they did not acquire their wealth by the usual two ways.

Like John D. Rockefeller, Warren Buffett is famous for his frugal lifestyle. He takes great pride in watching his money.

The rich are rich because they know the value of the dollar. They know that each dollar could be the seed that develops into a money tree, so they seldom miss the opportunity to save money. They are tracking their money through more and more detailed "Schedule A's." They are continuously planting money trees.

Take a lesson from the people who are in the top 20 percent. Spend less than what you earn. Spending is easy and gets us into many difficulties. Spending only for what is vital is a habit that requires development. As Benjamin Franklin noted: "Beware of little expenses; a small leak will sink a great ship."

Benjamin Franklin had another good way of reminding us of the fundamental power of saving: "A penny saved is a penny earned." Our parents said that a lot when we were growing up during the great depression.

As a retired surgeon, I have very few opportunities to increase my earned income. Still, it is not too late to assemble more money for investments by saving—even for me.

For example, senior citizen discounts and discounts to active service military personnel and veterans are excellent ways to save money for investing. I like visiting a Subway for lunch, and I have learned that you can get a 10 per cent senior citizen discount. I have also learned that these discounts do not come automatically. You have to ask for them each time you make a purchase. Often, you have to ask for the discount before the clerk begins to use the cash register.

We buy our groceries at a local Harris Teeter grocery store. Our weekly bill is approximately $150. Over a year, this adds up to almost $8,000. (52 x $150 = $7800). Harris Teeter gives a 5% discount to senior citizens who shop on Thursday. 5% of $7800 is $390. That is enough to purchase 10 shares of Coca-Cola stock or 4 shares of Exxon each year. With dividend reinvestment and compounding, the amount will soon be substantial.

Of course, you have to set the money aside for investment at the time that you save it.

OVERSPENDING CAN CREATE OPPORTUNITIES FOR LENDERS TO EARN SHOCKING PROFITS.

It is very costly to overdraw your bank account. For example, consider Sally's case. Sally was busy buying new clothes for her three children and overdrew her checking account by $24. The bank charged her a $36 fee. She corrected her account 2 days later and paid the $36-dollar fee. The effect of this transaction is that she was charged $36 for a loan of $24 for 2 days. 36/24 equals 1.5, which represents 150 per cent interest for a 2-day loan. There are 182.5 2-day periods in one year. 182.5 times 150 equals 27,375% interest, on an annual basis. No one can think that such a charge is fair, but lenders impose such charges every day.

The lesson here is that lenders exploit every moment of weakness or lack of discipline to earn inflated profits. Don't let them!

Take action:

1. Is there a discount that you can take advantage of? Try saving the money from that discount and putting that money towards an investment.

2. Have you been penalized lately by a bank or credit card or other lender? Calculate the annual cost of the money they lent you. What can you do to avoid this kind of penalty in the future?

15

Keeping Track Takes Discipline

"We are what we repeatedly do; excellence, then, is not an act but a habit."

—ARISTOTLE

I t is essential to continuously balance your cash accounts. There are three steps to balancing these accounts. Bank reconciliation is the name of the process.

The first step is adjusting the balance per bank. The second step is adjusting the balance per book. The third step is comparing the adjusted balances. There is a general rule for making these adjustments. The general rule is "put it where it isn't."

In adjusting the balance stated on the bank statement, it may be necessary to add deposits in transit, deduct outstanding checks, and add or deduct bank errors.

In adjusting the balance stated in your checkbook, it may be necessary to deduct bank service charges, deduct NSF checks and fees, deduct check printing charges, add interest earned, add notes receivable collected by the bank, and add or deduct errors in your cash account.

Brokerage accounts are balanced in the same manner. The brokerage account may have items somewhat different than the bank such as dividends and maintenance fees but in general you are comparing the brokerage account with the account you personally maintain.

After you have adjusted the two balances, they should match. If they don't, the usual cause is that you have failed to accurately track one or more of your transactions. Banks and brokerages do make errors. If you find one, act immediately. Call the bank or the brokerage house, be polite but be sure that the error is corrected. In this day and age, there may also be a possibility of identity theft.

The first time you reconcile a bank account, you should do it by hand, with a sheet of graph paper. But once you have done it a few times and understand how it works, you will find that there are many computerized products that would help walk you through the reconciliation process, such as Quicken. Once you move to double-entry bookkeeping, you will use more complex programs.

But remember: the farther you get from the written Schedule A, in your handwriting, the farther you get from the personal awareness you need of how each dollar is spent.

Professional accountants will often balance their books each day. Balance your accounts frequently, but never less than once a month.

Take Action: Balance your checking account. What can you do to make this process easier next month. For example, wouldn't it have been easier if all transactions had been properly entered at the time they were made? Isn't that a bit like following the Flying Cloud diet?

16

Doubling Your Money

"How to double your money: Fold it over once and put it back in your pocket."

--JIM DODDS

Mary had an uncle who taught her how to play chess. He told her that an Indian mathematician invented the game hundreds of years ago.

The mathematician's King learned the game and liked it so well he wanted to reward the gentlemen for his discovery. He told the mathematician to name his reward. The mathematician requested that grains of wheat be placed on the chessboard. One grain on the first square, two grains on the second square, four grains on the next square and a continuing doubling of the grains on each square until all 64 squares were covered.

The king agreed without hesitation and ordered the mathematician his reward. His agents soon appeared and warned the king to change the terms of the reward. There was not enough grain in the kingdom to cover the reward.

Mary, (Remember Mary?) has begun to feel badly about how far ahead of John she has gotten in life. She decided to explain compounding to John, but John was having a hard time comprehending the details. Remembering the story about chess she told him she had a problem for him to solve. He would need his scientific calculator to facilitate some of the mathematics involved.

In the problem, she described a hypothetical saver named Peter. Peter had found a way to double his money. Peter had one dollar and was able to double it every day for one week. Mary asks John: "How much money does Peter have at the end of the week?" John checked the mathematics on his scientific calculator, 2, x to the y power 7. $128 is the correct amount.

Peter was able to continue doubling his money. How much did Peter have at the end of the second week? Again John used his scientific calculator: 2, x to the y power 14. $16,384.

Without difficulty Peter continued to double his money for another week. How much money did Peter have at the end of the third week? He had 2, x to the y power 21 dollars. The number on the scientific calculator showed this to be $2,097,152.

Peter's friends were amazed. He continued doubling his money for another week. How much money did Peter have at the end of the fourth week? He had 2, x to the y power 28 which was $268,435,456. But this was December and December has 31 days. How much money did Peter have at the end of the month of December? He had 2, x to the y power 31 which is $2,147,483,648.

Now, for Mary's question. "Which period of time was most productive?" John was alert. He knew that the last three days were by far the most productive period of time.

Mary was happy that John could see that the longer the period of time, the greater the reward. That is exactly what happens in compounding.

THE RULE OF 72

This financial rule states that if you divide 72 by the annual rate of return, you can determine the number of years it will take your investment to double in value.

When using the rule of 72, treat percentages as whole numbers. Thus, if you earn a 1% rate of return, as you might earn in your Bank of America savings account, it will take 72 years (72 divided by 1) for your money to double. On the other hand, if you earned 18%, a conservative estimate of what Bank of America might earn on $1,000 charged on your credit card, it will take only 4 years (72÷18) for the Bank to double its money.

Doubling is an important concept in compounding. It is related to time, interest rate, and the number of periods of compounding that occur each year.

In 2016 Warren Buffett increased his wealth by $11.8 billion dollars. Warren Buffett compounds his money. You can see that he has been compounding for quite some time.

Take action: Figure out your overall percentage rate of return for your investments. How long will it take you to double your money? How can you reduce that period?

17

The Abacus: Touching and Seeing Your Money

"One machine can do the work of 50 ordinary men. No machine can do the work of one extraordinary man."

—ANONYMOUS

Most of us allow financial transactions to take place all around us without fully understanding them. It is similar to the way we watch television without understanding how the signal and the electricity are delivered, or how the set creates the picture. Our government incurs trillions of dollars of liabilities even though most of the people who make those decisions cannot even comprehend the concept of a trillion.

We have a desire to believe that financial success, like good health, appears somewhat naturally. Those who have financial success are often quite dismissive about the hard work that was necessary to attain it, wanting to create an image of brilliance.

If you study the lives of financially successful people, however, you will find that they understand the complexities of financial transactions, and they can see the effect of various transactions in a visual way.

Throughout this book, I have urged you to adopt the discipline to have a daily tactile awareness of what is happening to your money, by making entries in a journal. I have tried to teach you the compounding equation, so that you can visually understand how its various variables can affect what you pay or earn. Another trick is to use cash instead of credit cards so you can visually see how much you are spending.

Our emphasis on computers and efficiency has caused us to lose the experience of visually seeing the dollars we spend.

One way I have tried to teach my children to have a visual appreciation for the way numbers work is to teach them to use the abacus. It's not really that hard, and as you get used to it, it produces numerous benefits. My son Raphael, who has learned the abacus well, says that it produces an array of benefits, including the improvement of intelligence and brain development, concentration, academic performance, dexterity and confidence.

Take Action: You can buy an abacus conveniently on the Internet for less than $20. Try using it instead of a calculator.

18

The Magic Words

A Hair, they say, divides the False and True;
Yes; and a single Alif were the clue,
Could you but find it, to the Treasure-house,
And peradventure to the master too.

--OMAR KHAYYÁM
(PERSIAN POET, PHILOSOPHER,
MATHEMATICIAN, AND ASTRONOMER)

This book has been devoted to showing you how the difference between being rich or being poor may rest on a very simple mathematical formula. Do you remember the magic words? *A equals P times (1 + r/n) to the nt power.*

The compounding formula is the hair that divides the false and true. It is an Alif (the first letter of the alphabet) that leads to the treasure house and peradventure to the master too. Eight people who have focused on this formula now own the same wealth as half of the world's population.

Start today. Never allow the event of the moment to blind your vision of the future. Try to save at least one dollar each day. Invest these dollars carefully and watch them grow into giant money trees.

Try living by this rule: Whenever you enter a transaction that involves the compounding equation, make sure you are on the "A" side of the equation.

JOHN MAKES AN INVESTMENT

Let us finish on a happy note. John has had an epiphany. He has spent time improving his financial literacy. He is now on the A side of the compounding equation.

John has saved his money and has purchased a $10,000 investment that pays 8 per cent interest quarterly. How much money will John have at the end of one year? The elements of the equation should be familiar to you by now:

A equals 10,000 x (1 plus .08/4) to the 1 x 4 power.

A equals $ 10,824.32

John will earn $824.32 this year for his investment. Not a bad rate of return. He will double his money in nine years. Kind of like the returns Mary used to earn.

OPEN SESAME!

Growth is a survival mechanism. "Grow or die!" I have often told myself.

The idea for this book came from my own story of survival, but the title of this book comes from a story of survival that was framed inside another story of survival.

In 1704, a French archaeologist named Antoine Galland translated a Syrian manuscript of what we now know as *The Thousand and One Arabian Nights.* The manuscript told the story of an unhappy king, Shahryar. The world had turned dark for Shahryar as the result of a betrayal by his wife, whom he had executed. He had taken to consorting with a new virgin each night, and killing the poor girls in the morning. A brave young woman named Scheherazade was selected to be the King's next unfortunate companion. Scheherazade asked for permission to tell a story, and she just kept telling it. When morning came, the story was not yet done. And the King said "I am not going to kill her until I hear the rest of the story."

As it turned out, Scheherazade knew many stories, and she survived for a thousand nights retelling them. Enchanted, the King married her. Scheherazade's is a remarkable story of survival by clever wit and learning. She saved many lives, including her own.

As one of the many stories told by Scheherazade, Galland included the story of "*Ali Baba and the Forty Thieves.*" The story was not in the Syrian manuscript Galland was translating. He claimed to have heard the story from a monk. Some people think he made it up.

In the story, Ali Baba is a humble woodcutter who comes across a group of forty thieves in the forest. He hides behind a tree while he sees them going in and out of a cave, which their leader opens by saying "Open Sesame." When the thieves depart, Ali Baba goes in and finds piles of gold and priceless merchandise, which, he thinks, must be the product of centuries of larceny. Ali Baba helps himself to some of the gold. While he tries to be quiet about his secret, his brother Qasim learns the secret and goes to the cave, but forgets the magic words. The thieves kill Qasim. Realizing their secret has been found out, the thieves search out Ali Baba. Although they make numerous attempts kill Ali Baba, they are foiled his slave Marjana, another young woman who engineers the survival of herself and others through great skill and cleverness. To reward Marjana, Ali Baba arranges for his son to marry her.

As the story ends, Ali Baba takes his son to the cave. There he teaches his son the secret of how to enter it by saying "Open Sesame." He teaches his son to use his wealth with restraint. They resolve to pass on the secret of Open Sesame to their descendants.

There is no major expense in sharing information in this book with your family, friends and associates. There are many people who are born, live their lives and die without ever having heard of compounding.

Now that I have told you the magic words of the compounding formula, I would ask you to pass on the secret just as Ali Baba passed on the magic words of "Open Sesame" to his son and his resourceful wife Marjana.

Memorize the formula and teach it to at least twelve of your friends. And ask them to teach the formula to at least twelve of their friends.

Don't stop there. If you are good at money-management, pass your skills on to your children, grandchildren, nieces, and nephews. That's what I am trying to do with this book.

You become what you think about.

You think about what you think about.

What you think about you bring about.

Draw in a deep breath.

Go for it. Give it a try.

59361959R00042

Made in the USA
San Bernardino, CA
04 December 2017